Care for Caregivers

Poetry of Support and Understanding

BY

Judith Morse Braunfeld

Dedication

Dedicated to Mammy

Acknowledgements

I would like to acknowledge my husband Peter for his wisdom and patience.

I want more time before the door closes.
Can't we talk more about the good times?
When you go into that place,
I'll be so alone.

You got so angry yesterday,
I only tried to help.
Why do you feel so smothered?
I do it because I love you so.

I thought we had more time.
What fun we always had.
Why did it end so soon?
Instead of tomorrows,
I'll only have yesterdays.

The new normal is so odd.
You were always on the go, doing for others.
Now they are doing for you.

Please don't be so sad.
I know it isn't fair.
The good times that we had,
still aren't over.

These times are hard for both of us.
So please don't always make a fuss.
I try to think before I act,
but often I am short on tact.

I saw you fall, but I couldn't help.
Then while you lay there all I could do is hold your hand.
I wanted to carry you to safety.
At least my love surrounded you.

Incontinence is the cruelest indignity.
I've heard you say it out loud.
But when it happens to you,
it is different isn't it?

Oh Mother please remember me.
You once brushed my hair.
Now when I brush yours,
your shy smile makes me think you do remember.

Do you want to wear the green dress or the blue?
Would you like the jello or the pudding?
If you make simple choices,
it helps you feel you are still in control.

Please don't cry Dear,
you know it hurts me so.
I wish I could help you laugh again.
It was such a sweet sound.

Salt!
What problems it creates between us.
When the doctor says no, then why do you fuss?
If you say "I'd rather die than go without", how should I act when you begin to pout?

It must be hard to lose control of what your hands will do.
You drop, and twist and try again, yet it slides away from you.
Is it like eating spaghetti with a spoon?

Sometimes I wonder if I can keep going.
It isn't just he that needs me.
What about the ballgame and the prom?
If only I had a double!

I'm coming! I'm coming!
When you call me from the other room,
your question vanishes in the air.
I run back and forth to your calls all day long.
Maybe an intercom is the answer.

If friends would remember you can't eat candy and cookies.
I feel guilty being the food police, and you resent me for it.
Maybe I should make a "Do Not Feed" sign.

Come on! Come on!
My mind says to me.
She is moving as fast as she can
she says.
How can everything take so long?
When she used to be the head of the crowd?

When you complain that everything hurts, I feel bad, but how can I help? Perhaps when I am 86, I'll understand.

Having trouble sleeping again?
Is your brain filling with thoughts?
I remember when I couldn't sleep,
you'd sing me a lullaby.

We bought the special lamp that advertised, "No Glare".
Then we got the big magnifying glass that attached to it.
Next came the large print books.
Don't cry Sweetheart, I'll read to you.

When our little great-grandchildren visit they mean well.
The littlest one hadn't seen false teeth,
and could hardly believe you could take them out.
She thinks you are a magician!

You used to enjoy going to the mall. I'd push your chair while you loved to people watch, after lunch at our favorite place.
Now you just want to go home.

It was so hard to put away the lovely scatter rugs we bought in Turkey,
so long ago.
But we were told they might cause a fall.
And we have always been obedient.

I know you hate being pushed about like some big baby, of course it makes you mad.
But I know you hate being indoors more.
So how about I get you a sporty scarf or a red hat?
You'll show 'em!

Remember when I was so afraid of thunderstorms that you would climb into my bed to calm me until I fell asleep?
Where can I go now when I am afraid?

I've told you a hundred times to
slow down or you'll fall.
Well now it's finally happened.
Is it like when you used to yell at us,
"I've told you a hundred times"?
It does sound familiar.

Nothing seems to please you.
Food isn't hot enough.
The shower is too hot. The TV is too quiet,
but the children are too noisy.
If only we could all be on the same wavelength.
It sure would make life simple.

When is long enough? What is not too heavy?
Where do you want this?
Who can help you Dear?
My new life is filled with questions.

It is 11:00 and you ought to be in bed.
I only care because you said you felt tired all day.
You were never a night owl, when did that change?
I can no longer understand you, yet I always did.

I know you hate these elastic stockings, even though they help so much.
Remember the girdles you always wore when I was small?
Isn't it too bad that when you got to give up one, the other came along?

I wait for you as you waited for me.
You are always so patient.
But I can't say I am.
If only you had passed that patience on to me.

I admire your spunk.
This low protein diet must be awful,
but you don't complain.
When I brought you those hard
candies, you spread them out on
your covers and exclaimed
"these are my jewels".

I remember when the days flew by,
Don't you?
Now it seems each hour is too long.
What new problem surface today?
What is the disease de jour?
There are no answers.

Should I tell you that Dad isn't coming, because he died last year?
Do I make believe I am your beloved sister, gone so many years ago?
I guess it's best to go along with you.
There's no harm in it.

You were doing so well until you fell. Everyone used to remark that at 90 you put us all to shame.
It seems that old bones seldom mend.
Do hearts?

Now that I got you the magnetic closing shirts, you can dress yourself again.
I see it pleases you to be in control.

Taking a shower is so scary.
I get the water set and then you step in.
Getting back out is such a challenge.

I think the nurse is in love with you.
Have you noticed that she flirts with you every week?
She must see the charms.
I discovered it long ago.

I just bought a gadget that will help us.
It is a sort of rubber triangle.
I'll hold one side and you the other.
Now I can finally help pull you up.

Remember the wonderful swing, on the back porch?
We could have sat there for hours and enjoyed the garden.

Do you miss Dusty too?
What a sweet little dog she was.
Too bad we can't have a pet here.

Let's talk about one of the cruises we so enjoyed.
If we could sail again, where would you go?

I know you miss your garden Mom, and working in it.
At least we can make a window box with all of your favorites.

It's been so hard today,
to hear you lost your friend.
Could you think about your fun times?
And then say goodbye?

It is so nice to cuddle together.
Even though we have done so for so long.
Somehow now it seems sweeter.

I was just thinking about our very first date.
Our conversation went on so long, they told us they needed to close!

What should I do on days when you feel so low?
Do you want words of support?
Or should I just hug you?

I am going to push your chair outside.
Sometimes I think we need to go out more.
How about you?

What do you miss most about the old days?
For me, I guess it is the spontaneity. It was great to just go when the spirit moved us.

Isn't it exciting that our grandson is getting married?
We remember when he was a sweet little boy.
Now we can watch them develop into a special family.

Your blood pressure goes up and down.
We never know what to expect.
Even though you take your meds, we are often concerned.

The cleaning woman thinks you are beautiful.
She even said you were.
I've told people that for years!

Have you noticed that after you wear your hearing aids all day and finally take them out, it seems like you hear nothing?

Daddy, I know how much you worry about having enough money. It probably comes from when your family didn't.
But now you have plenty to meet your needs.

I'm glad you like the new magnetic closing shirts I bought.
Now you can feel more in control.

About The Author

Judith Braunfeld was born in 1937 and grew up in the Boston suburb of Newton. Judy, as she is known by her friends, was especially close to her grandmother, "Mammy." She developed her love of music, singing with Mammy and had her first solo at age 8.

Judy's deep relationship with her grandma fostered a love for the company and wisdom of elders. After a divorce in her thirties, she went back to school and graduated from the University of Illinois (U of I) with a degree in Gerontology, and a minor in voice. During this time she met her current husband, Peter, and they created a blended family with her three children, Alison, Peter, and Kristen, and Peter's two children, Ken and David. Alison is now a special ed teacher, Peter is an actor, Kristen is a minister, Ken is a city planner, and David is in sales.

Over the years, Judy has worked at various nursing homes and was the Community Coordinator on Aging for the city of Indianapolis. She also ran a student foundation at the U of I, through which she created a women's shelter, a food coop, and multiple programs that brought students and older adults together. She has spoken on aging to audiences across the country, including New York's, Chautauqua and the U of I. She also ran her own consulting business serving aging parents and their children, for forty years before retiring. Her love of singing has continued throughout her life. She performed in many well known groups, her favorite being the Paul Hill Chorale.

The genesis for this book began when she lectured at the Chautauqua Women's Club on, "Caring for Caregivers." These poems come from her years of supporting seniors and their caregivers as they face the emotional challenges related to aging and her personal experiences with her husband, Peter who is now 92.

Judith and Peter

Judith and her children

www.ingramcontent.com/pod-product-compliance
Lightning Source LLC
Chambersburg PA
CBHW041642090426
42736CB00034BA/5